COOL COMPUTING JOBS

APP DESIGN

NANCY DICKMANN

Published in 2024 by
KidHaven Publishing, an Imprint of Greenhaven Publishing, LLC
2544 Clinton St., Buffalo, NY 14224

Text and Editor: Nancy Dickmann
Children's Publisher: Anne O'Daly
Design Manager: Keith Davis
Designer and Illustrator: Supriya Sahai
Picture Manager: Sophie Mortimer

Picture Credits
Key: t=top, b=bottom, c=center, l=left, r=right
Interior: Shutterstock: B Bernard 20; Chaosamran Studio 13, 15; Creativa Images 8; Foxy burrow 17; fizkes 23; Gorodenkoff 22; g-stockstudio 11; Halfpoint 9, 29t; Insta photos 27; George JMC Little 12; mangpor2004 25; Maridav 10; oatawa 4, 29b; Chansom Pantip 7; Phil's Mommy 26; Aleksandr Potashev 5; Prostock-studio 18; Regissercom 21; Konstantin Savusia 16; seewhatmitchsee 19, 28, Nazlin Sha 24; Oleksandr Zamuruiev 14. United States Government: GPS.gov Image Library 6.

Cataloging-in-Publication Data

Names: Dickmann, Nancy.
Title: App design / Nancy Dickmann.
Description: Buffalo, New York : KidHaven Publishing, 2024. |
Series: Cool computing jobs | Includes glossary and index.
Identifiers: ISBN 9781534546448 (pbk.) | ISBN 9781534546455 (library bound) | ISBN 9781534546462 (ebook)
Subjects: LCSH: Mobile apps--Juvenile literature. | Mobile apps--Vocational guidance--Juvenile literature. | Application software--Development--Juvenile literature. | Computer programming--Juvenile literature.
Classification: LCC QA76.59 D534 2024 | DDC 005.35--dc23

Manufactured in the United States of America

CPSIA compliance information: Batch #CW24KH: For further information contact Greenhaven Publishing LLC at 1-844-317-7404.

Please visit our website, www.greenhavenpublishing.com.
For a free color catalog of all our high-quality books, call toll free 1-844-317-7404 or fax 1-844-317-7405.

Find us on

CONTENTS

01

WHAT IS AN APP?

Smartphones are amazing! Their apps are a big part of why they're so useful.

Some apps cost money to download, but others are free.

Cell phones, tablets, and computers all run apps. "App" is short for "application." An app is a piece of software that lets a device do a specific task. There are millions to choose from. Some apps come preloaded on a phone or other device.

Kinds of Apps

There is an app for practically everything! Some send messages, while others help you manage your money. There are calculator apps, alarm clock apps, and music apps. There are also games, calendars, and apps for editing photos.

Some apps are silly but fun. There is one that adds cats to your photos!

Weather apps tell you if you'll need an umbrella.

01

{ }

HOW AN APP WORKS

We often take apps for granted. Have you ever wondered how they work?

Apps on phones and tablets use touch screens. You tap, swipe, or pinch to use the app. It's how you give the app information and tell it what to do. That's called input. Sometimes you need to enter text. A keyboard pops up on the screen for you to tap.

Satellites in space can provide input for an app. They help it figure out its location.

Many phones have settings and apps to help people with disabilities, such as voice controls for people with vision impairment.

Signals

Some apps, like an alarm clock, don't need an internet connection. Others, such as banking apps, do. The app needs to contact your bank to get information about your account. It sends and receives signals. It can do this using Wi-Fi or using a cellular netwok.

Tall cell towers send and receive the signals that a cell phone uses.

A BRIGHT IDEA

Which apps do you use? Have you ever thought about designing your own?

All apps start as an idea. Many apps solve problems or make tasks easier for the user. For example, an app might help people order takeout. It might provide a new way to share photos and videos. A good app idea is unique. It doesn't copy other apps.

Some apps help translate foreign words on restaurant menus.

Who's It For?

Every app has a target audience—the people who are most likely to use it. A simple game app might be targeted at children. An app for booking flights might be for businesspeople. When planning an app, it's important to think about what the audience will want from it.

Apps come with age ratings. They show which ages the app is appropriate for.

Fitness apps are targeted at people who like to exercise.

01

{ }

DEVELOPMENT TEAMS

Creating an app is a big job. It usually takes a team to do it.

A product manager might have a plan for a new kind of travel app.

A product manager often takes the lead. They are in charge of strategy. They think about the target audience. They analyze other similar apps. Then, they figure out what will make their app stand out. What features will it need? How will they sell it?

Project Managers

A project manager is a bit different. Once the app is planned, they make sure the work gets done. They organize the other team members. They create budgets and schedules, then make sure that everyone sticks to them. A project manager needs good communication and leadership skills.

A project manager makes sure that each step of the app's development is finished at the right time.

Regular team meetings let a project manager check everyone's progress.

PLANNING THE APP

You have your idea. You know your audience. Now it's time to plan the app!

App development teams think about how customers will use the app. What features will they want? How should they be organized? The team sketches out a plan. It's like a flowchart. It shows the steps that users will take as they move through the app.

A good shopping app makes it easy to compare prices, choose an item, and pay for it.

A graphic designer creates the app icon that appears on a phone's home screen.

A graphic designer might sketch in pencil, then use design software for the finished version.

Words and Pictures

A graphic designer creates the look of an app. They choose colors and styles. A children's game might have bright colors, while a luxury travel app looks sophisticated. Apps need words too! A copywriter writes clear text for the user that matches their audience.

EASY TO USE

A good app is easy to use. Getting it right takes a lot of work.

A game app for young children must be simple, with symbols instead of written directions.

Have you ever gotten annoyed at an app that's hard to navigate? The UI/UX designer is in charge of making sure this doesn't happen. UI/UX stands for "user interface/user experience." UI/UX designers plan menus, buttons, and other navigation features.

Spotting Patterns

The UI/UX designer puts together a wireframe of the app. This is a very basic version, like a blueprint for a building. It doesn't have finished graphics or animation, but it shows what will appear on each screen and how you get from one screen to another.

UI/UX designers show their wireframes to typical users to get feedback.

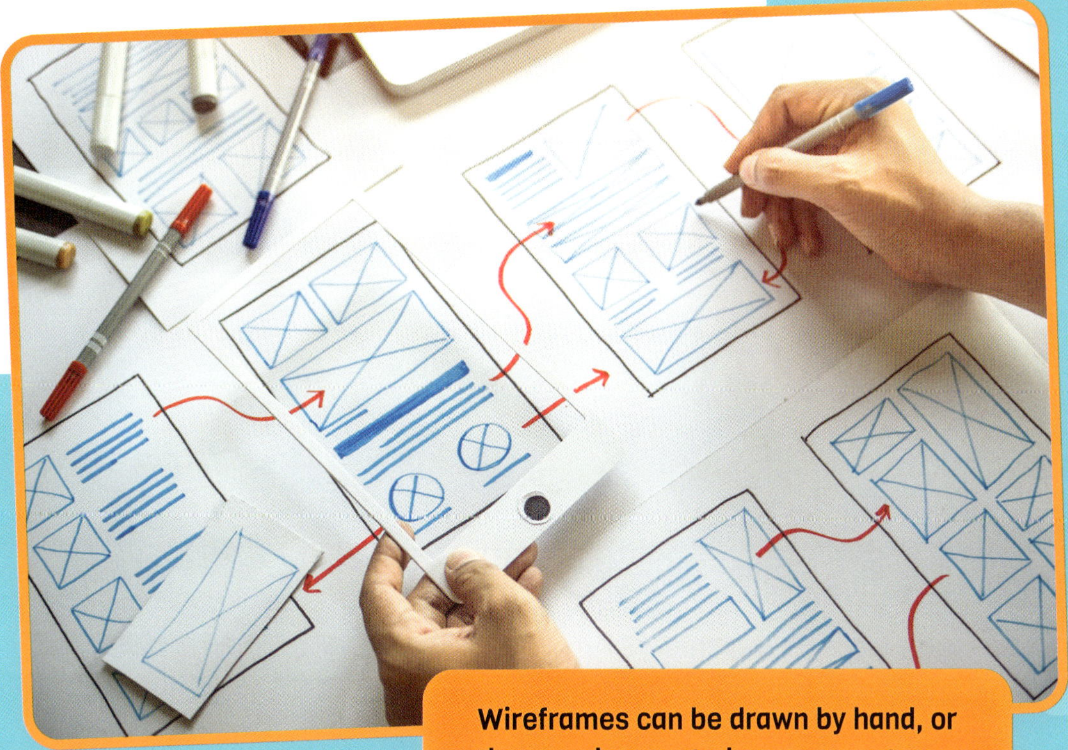

Wireframes can be drawn by hand, or they can be created on a computer.

01

APP DEVELOPERS

The finished wireframe must be turned into a working app. Time to get coding!

An app is a program—a set of instructions that tell a computer what to do. It's a bit like the instructions for building a toy model, just a lot more complicated! An app developer writes the code for an app.

App developers use software that shows how their code will work on a phone.

Which Platform?

Most phones and tablets use one of two operating systems—Android or iOS. Apps often come in two versions, one for each system. They are coded in different ways. Many app developers specialize in one or the other. Others are able to work with both systems.

A simple game app might have 50,000 lines of code. More complicated apps have millions!

Developers code apps so that they will automatically resize to fit your device's screen.

01

{ }

PROGRAMMING LANGUAGES

An app's code has to be in a language that a computer will understand.

Computer code lists commands in the right order, like the steps in a recipe.

Code is a system of words, numbers, and symbols that form instructions. Just like people speak different languages, coding uses different languages too. App developers may need to know several programming languages. They choose the one that's best for the app.

A code or system that uses ones and zeroes is called binary.

Do You Understand?

Each programming language has its own terms and symbols, and rules for using them. However, a computer only understands ones and zeroes. These numbers represent electrical signals that are either off or on. The computer reads each coded character as a string of ones and zeroes.

Languages such as Java, Kotlin, Swift, and Objective-C are often used for making apps.

{ }

01

BACKEND DEVELOPERS

What you see when you use an app is just the surface.

It takes the work of many people to create an amazing concert.

Have you ever been to the theater or to a concert? The performance looks smooth and polished, but behind the scenes, there are lots of people hard at work. They operate the lights and sound system. They make the costumes. They set up the stage.

An app is controlled from a central server like these, which send and receive information.

Behind the Scenes

It's the same with an app. A backend developer is in charge of coding the parts of an app that users don't see. They control how it stores or shares data. They also control how a shopping app takes payments and keeps your payment information safe.

Backend developers make it easy for an app on your phone to communicate with a server.

TEST IT OUT!

The app is coded. Is it ready to release?

Computer hackers look for flaws that let them break into an app to steal data.

Customers want an app that works well. If it drains their battery or uses too much memory, they'll delete it. That's why app developers do a lot of testing. They want to find and fix any problems before the app is released. For example, they make sure the app is secure and safe from hackers.

Checking It Out

A QA engineer is in charge of testing. “QA” stands for “quality assurance.” Sometimes they test manually. They use the app like a customer would. There is also software that helps with testing. A QA engineer writes code to tell it what to look for.

QA engineers make sure that an app works well on different devices.

App companies also test an app with real-life users to see if they like it.

KEEPING IT UPDATED

There's still work to do after the app is launched!

If you use apps, you already know that sometimes you need to download an update. This is a new version of an app. It's often mostly the same as the old version, but any glitches should be fixed. It will also be updated to work on the latest operating system.

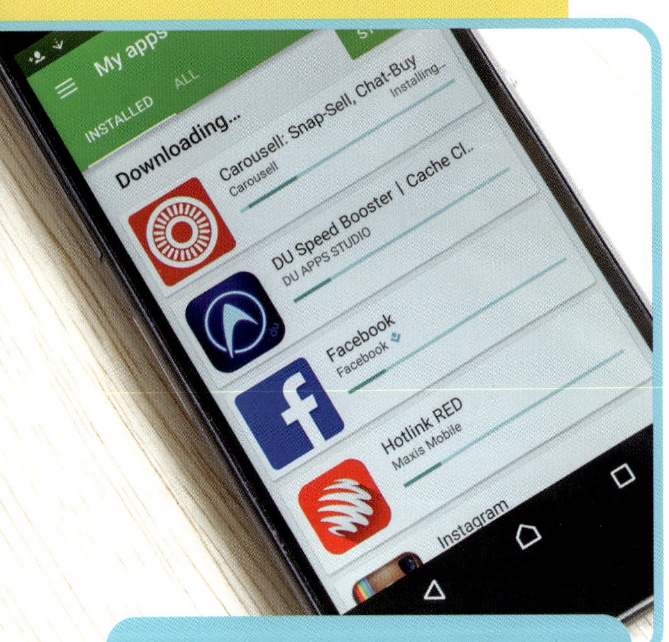

Once you've bought an app, the updates are usually free.

For a big update, app developers might decide to add new features to the app.

Big and Small

Each version of an app has a number, such as 5.2.3. Only a big change in the app will change the first digit. The second digit shows smaller changes, and the third shows tiny bug fixes. This makes it easy to see if you're using the latest version.

Most popular apps are updated several times a year. This keeps them safe and secure.

HOW TO PREPARE

Making apps is a great career. It's not too early to start preparing for a job in this field!

The more you practice coding, the better you'll get.

App developers and backend developers do the main coding for an app, but most members of the team will know at least a little coding. Coding is fun and easy to learn. Why not use a coding platform like Scratch to try to code a simple maze game?

Know Your Strengths

There are many different jobs in app design and development. Some of them use creativity, like a graphic designer. Others need coding skills, like a backend developer. A project manager needs to stay organized. Which job is the best match for your skills?

Apps are a big business. There are more than 100 billion app downloads a year!

Some kits let you build a robot and then make it move using code you write yourself.

QUIZ

Which job in app development is the best fit for you? Answer these questions and check your results at the end.

1. What do you think is the most important thing when hosting a party?

A. sending out invitations and starting on time

B. making sure everyone has a good time

C. following the recipes exactly to make great party food

2. How would you get involved with the school play?

A. I'd make a rehearsal schedule so that we're ready for the performance.

B. I'd design the programs so the audience knows what to expect.

C. I'd work backstage on scenery and lighting.

3. How do you spend your allowance?

A. I make a strict budget and stick to it.

B. I spend it on outings that I plan for my friends.

C. I'm saving up for a programmable robot kit.

4. What's your usual role in a group project at school?

A. making sure everyone knows their job and does it on time

B. creating an outline to make sure we meet the goals of the project

C. tech support

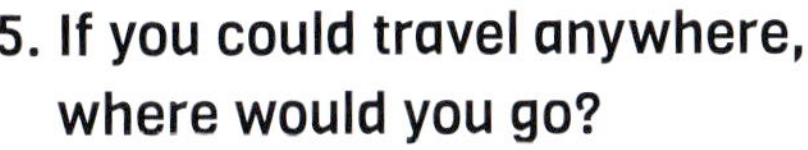

5. If you could travel anywhere, where would you go?

A. a cruise with a planned schedule of events

B. a favorite place I have been to before so I can plan an efficient and fun trip

C. a country where I can try out a new language

Add up your answers.

What did you get?

Mostly As: You could be a project manager. You're organized, you like working in a team, and you're good with schedules and budgets.

Mostly Bs: You could be a UI/UX designer. You like to plan things out and make them efficient, and you like to make people happy.

Mostly Cs: You could be an app developer. You like languages and have a good eye for detail—both important skills for coding. You also like working behind the scenes, so a backend developer might be a good fit for you.

GLOSSARY

analyze to study something in detail to find out what it is or how it works

budget a plan setting out how much money is available and how it will be spent

bug an error in a computer program or system

code a system of letters and symbols used as instructions for a computer

command an order or instruction given to a computer

data information in the form of facts or statistics that can be analyzed

flowchart a diagram that shows a step-by-step process through a system, often with arrows

icon a symbol that represents a computer application on a screen

input something that is put into a system, such as information that is sent to a computer

interface the way in which two things (such as a person and a computer) interact or communicate

navigate to find your way through something

operating system the program that controls a computer's basic functions and keeps its parts working together

program a set of coded instructions for a computer to follow

programming language a formal language designed to communicate instructions to a machine, especially a computer

server a computer that stores and sends out information to other computers

software programs that run on computers and perform certain functions

strategy a careful plan of how you will work toward a particular goal

touch screen a display screen that lets a user interact with a computer by touching areas on the screen

wireframe a very basic version of an app that shows how its menus, buttons, and screens are linked

FIND OUT MORE

Books

Hudak, Heather C. *Amazing App Developers***.** Minneapolis, MN: Checkerboard Library, 2018**.**

Kaul, Jennifer. *Inside Smartphones.* Minneapolis, MN: Core Library, 2019.

Lynn, Randy. *Coding Concepts for Kids: Learn to Code Without a Computer.* Emeryville, CA: Rockridge Press, 2020.

Woodcock, Jon. *Coding Games in Scratch: A Step-by-Step Visual Guide to Building Your Own Computer Games.* New York, NY: DK Children, 2019.

Websites

Go here to learn more about apps:
www.lifewire.com/what-are-apps-1616114

Learn more details about computer programming here:
www.dkfindout.com/uk/computer-coding/

This website has free online coding courses and activities:
studio.code.org/courses

This website will get you started coding in Scratch:
scratch.mit.edu

This video explains debugging:
www.bbc.com/bitesize/articles/ztkx6sg

Publisher's note to educators and parents: Our editors have carefully reviewed these websites to ensure that they are suitable for students. Many websites change frequently, however, and we cannot guarantee that a site's future contents will continue to meet our high standards of quality and educational value. Be advised that students should be closely supervised whenever they access the internet.

INDEX